Portraits of Drowning

Madeleine Dale grew up on Tamborine Mountain and now lives in Brisbane. She holds First-class Honours and a Masters in Creative Writing from the University of Queensland, where she is currently completing a PhD. Her first chapbook, *On Fire with Dangerous Cargo,* was published by Queensland Poetry in 2023. *Portraits of Drowning* is her first full-length collection.

THE ARTS QUEENSLAND THOMAS SHAPCOTT POETRY PRIZE SERIES

Lidija Cvetkovic *War Is Not the Season for Figs*
Jaya Savige *latecomers*
Nathan Shepherdson *Sweeping the Light Back into the Mirror*
Angela Gardner *Parts of Speech*
Sarah Holland-Batt *Aria*
Felicity Plunkett *Vanishing Point*
Rosanna Licari *An Absence of Saints*
Vlanes *Another Babylon*
Nicholas Powell *Water Mirrors*
Rachael Briggs *Free Logic*
David Stavanger *The Special*
Krissy Kneen *Eating My Grandmother: a grief cycle*
Stuart Barnes *Glasshouses*
Shastra Deo *The Agonist*
Rae White *Milk Teeth*
Anna Jacobson *Amnesia Findings*
Luke Best *Cadaver Dog*
Gavin Yuan Gao *At the Altar of Touch*
Janaka Malwatta *blackbirds don't mate with starlings*
Jarad Bruinstroop *Reliefs*

Madeleine **Dale**

Portraits of Drowning

UQP

First published 2024 by University of Queensland Press
PO Box 6042, St Lucia, Queensland 4067 Australia

University of Queensland Press (UQP) acknowledges the Traditional Owners and their custodianship of the lands on which UQP operates. We pay our respects to their Ancestors and their descendants, who continue cultural and spiritual connections to Country. We recognise their valuable contributions to Australian and global society.

uqp.com.au
reception@uqp.com.au

Copyright © Madeleine Dale 2024
The moral rights of the author have been asserted.

This book is copyright. Except for private study, research, criticism or reviews, as permitted under the Copyright Act, no part of this book may be reproduced, stored in a retrieval system, or transmitted in any form or by any means without prior written permission. Enquiries should be made to the publisher.

Cover design by Sandy Cull
Author photograph by Kate Lund
Typeset in 11.5/14 pt Adobe Garamond Pro by Post Pre-press Group, Brisbane
Printed in Australia by McPherson's Printing Group

Queensland Government University of Queensland Press is supported by the Queensland Government through Arts Queensland.

University of Queensland Press is assisted by the Australian Government through Creative Australia, its principal arts investment and advisory body.

A catalogue record for this book is available from the National Library of Australia.

ISBN 978 0 7022 6859 5 (pbk)
ISBN 978 0 7022 6987 5 (epdf)

University of Queensland Press uses papers that are natural, renewable and recyclable products made from wood grown in well-managed forests and other controlled sources. The logging and manufacturing processes conform to the environmental regulations of the country of origin.

*for Linda and Hilary Dale,
who let me dream*

Contents

I

The Poet in Water   3
Eleven Portraits of Drowning   4
The Fraser (I)   7
Piners   8
About Your Absence   9
Cicada Song   10
The War Artist   12
The Western Lewin's Rail   14
The Fraser (II)   15
Occlude   16
About cars and God   17
Coracle   19
Chandelle   21
The Great Auk   23
Open Letter to the Great Eastern Brood   25
Nocturne   26
Avarie   27

II

Sketch of a Man Drying His Hair After Nearly Drowning   31
Three Mornings   32
The Shallows Become the Shore   33
Crush Fracture   34
To the Silkworm   35

As Rachel, As Sarah   36
Automatica   38
As Sounding Brass   39
Okinawa Glass   40
The Cup-bearer   41
Sketch of a Man at Harvest Time   42
Salt Rose, Topaz   43
Anchor Watch   44
The Pearl as Immune Response   45
Catch Limits and Closures   46
Taking Men off the Ice   47
Hamadryad   48
The Flood of '28   49
Submerged Hazards   50

III

The Memorial   53
Came Back Wrong   54
Because the River Freezes   55
Give Andromache a Knife   56
Northwest Augury   57
Cephalophore   58
Arsenic in Soil   59
Pesto   60
The Deer   62
FrogID   63
Underwater Archaeology   65
Resuscitation Annie   66
Sad Girls' Dictionary   69
Fiat, for Three Voices   70
Meet Me in the Car Park   72

Providence 73
Kleinkill 76

Notes 77
Acknowledgements 83

I

The figure reclines on the left shoulder and slightly backwards; the head rests on the ground amid the flowing masses of its long hair, which are as if the sea had left them so …

– Anon., 'The Shelley Memorial'

The Poet in Water
Lerici, 1822

Imagine Mary, waiting ten days by the yellow house
as if waiting for inspiration –
for the same raw-breeze muse who turns oak leaves
over and breaks windfall fruit from its branch.

When his body fetches shore, it can't be carried
inside or swung onto the kitchen table like an apple bough
whose last white flowers film wet skin. The bloom
of his palms has fallen apart, like cheap printer's paper;

a week of storm-blow has salted the stucco walls,
and through lit windows
a novel's slow sorrow was seen turning on the rug,
stoking up the fire in search of story's sparks.

But death, like a poem, came to him suddenly.
So fast there was no time to cork the wine or strip off shirts.
So fast he broke the spine of *Lamia*,
which was fished from his pocket, bent in two.

Eleven Portraits of Drowning

A hundred and ten millimetres in a single day.

Local bridges were cut quickly –
a decade ago, they still followed fording paths,
low-slung concrete kissed by shallow creeks.

It used to seem good luck to be shut in by water,
to seek alternate routes   miss appointments.

~

A list of drowning victims:

Natalie   found spine-up in the Pacific,
                 the downed bird of her jacket snatched
                 from its element.

Two men argued politics over her absence;
the coroner wrung water from her clothes
– and no-one could clear it from her lungs.

~

A river in flood is spoken like a pregnancy:
swollen swelling hungry banks broken broken waters.

Our words for birth are our words for fear.

~

Ophelia's
Two men found upright in
grave –
she swallowed her death in the dry impasse
between scenes five and six. Men argued

over her mind as she stepped out of the text
and into the water.

~

A search for drowned women:

drowning porn videos drowning underwater videos
drowning watch women drowning porn videos for free.

~

It's not the water.

~

The Australian Border Deaths Database:

Interdiction at sea   *2 women*   *4 adult women*
1 female (pregnant)   *three female children*
Unknown woman   *small number of women*

142 women.

~

An immigration minister is sixty per cent water.

~

Christina   in nine inches of fire-stung stream,
wet eyelids, soot skin.
Two men argued over the story –

and no-one remembers who lifted her out of the water
or swept a billow of soaked hair from her temple.

~

Ruin takes record for challenge; the interior
of any lung is a ready site of inundation.

What to carry? When to tie back our hair
and place our names in a water-tight tub?

A coal baron is sixty per cent water.

~

Three point two millimetres in a single year. Two men
argue over how high the Pacific will take a tidemark

on a sitting-room wall   on a high-rise   a feed-shed
over a field   a river system   a freeway   a damp shirt.

A woman sits down in a flood of salt.

The Fraser (I)

I was thinking of logs in the Fraser River,
their bright skins rolling up, up and out of the salmon run –
a whole pine lot stripped and turned sideways,
slung against the booms like a tapped box of pencils.
A jam-man goes trunk to trunk, poling out an order;
in another imagining, he carries dynamite
and the rough drive to use it. Now, fingernails
of bark flake into the current and are rushed away
like rafts of dead pollen. Upstream, early morning
curdles on blue glass. Churches sell their air rights,
and the jam-man kneels to pray or eat,
to press against the dirt and give his sky a better price.
I was thinking of wild things and what we make of them.

Piners

Months to take a single Huon:
the pining work upstream,

dragging the body across
a wet, fractal language of moss.

Beech double in the black-
tea sheen of the Gordon,

fan along a dark slip
of shoredirt like terracotta swell

through glaze. Turned sideways,
I could step out of this elegy –

the folded couplets of land
and land's echo. A piner's

punt knifes the glass. The trees
belly alongside. Felled wood

floats – halved and made again
in the water's imagination.

About Your Absence

It's a divot in earth, a figure cut from cold cloth
in my passenger seat. It's what green ants carry
out of their cathedral mounds – the hollowing
instinct, for which I have no reason. Only
that the broad back of the mountain is held down
by its own heaviness – twenty-two million years
of missing the year before. Rabbit-rats and parrots.
Emptiness enlarging itself with a lip curled.

It's the fog bank cast down along the ridge,
solid as a second body. The clear-cuts stubbled
like stripes of hair shaved to stitch a wound.
You and the mountain have this in common:
a vanishing. The mountain and I have the loss
of our living things. Late grevillea coming apart
in pink loops. Your after-image ghosting
through teenage flooded gum. Certain graves
carried in the organs.

Cold air licks like breath against my damp skin.
If only there were a wound. If only there were
anything other than the green ants, hauling earth

                        to make more space.

Cicada Song

How great
the grief of them,

of ground that tallies
out small resurrections.

Blur of wings,
diaphanous fragments

skimming lost vowels,
a spring spent palm-

to-dirt, waiting out
buried adolescence.

For sap-roots & shed,
they slid

from a sentence
between consonants,

gone so long
my tongue forgot

how to turn the song
whole. I wake

in a chorus tree's
howl; discarded shells

rattle, their split backs
clawed up from burial.

They do not mean
to teach me hope

or dark soil's wayfare
– but how are you lost

to earth that yields
so much singing.

The War Artist

A friend who didn't enlist in '41, still waiting for the dragnet
of the draft to scoop him like so much seafish. Paid to sprawl
on the cold studio floor. Shivers. Smiles. Has never been
a painter's muse before. Drop sheet caught around his legs
for the sea, borrowed canvas slops – it's good enough
for a first study. Corn-pale lashes sweeping shut. A dead sailor.
Full of salt. The muffled shape at beach's end; the gut-shock
when a wave turns it and combers see the face,
like when a dog comes running and the prize in its mouth
is a drowned bird. Bit of bad providence. Old paint on the brush.
Dirty light from big ceiling panes bends down
to kiss the floor, his hair, the knuckles of one hand outflung
like a boxer spun and felled mid-swing. *Christ, kid, you look
dead.* It feels bad luck to paint him into it – bent knee,
head knocked to one side, yellow hair splashed on the concrete.
His hand opens and contracts, trying to catch the water, like
something twitching on its back. *Don't move yet* – but it's only
winter sun scraping itself raw on the roof, setting white bars
across his shins. Flare of bare skin where the shirt rucks. Easy
enough to picture the shore where he'll wash up. The drag
of a little tide that grabs his hair with insistent hands, pulls out sand
from under his side. Makes a pedestal in the shape of a body.
Skin shades on the palette, the colours of living flesh. He has to look
like he can still be saved. The point is to pick the boy up off the beach.
The point is to shut your mouth in the shops; don't share bad news
about meat that was once men. The blood will come later:
cadmium dabbed inside a torn elbow, clots riding the foam
where it eddies like lace. Salt air rots red paint black,
but these wounds will be poster-bright for years. Thousands

of flyers by the end: tattered ghosts in a grocer's window, a station.
The point is he'll board a ship in '44 and die in Holland,
where dirt will eat him like water. The point is when the news
comes, in an envelope the colour of old lemons and crushed lead,
you will have already given his body to the war. A canvas stacked
in a government corridor. The oil still wet. *Okay.*
You can get up now. Please.

The Western Lewin's Rail

Margaret River's reel becomes
four museum objects

split-bellied into tin buckets,
the hot mouth of a curator's cat.

At the doors of naturalists
and by institution docks

hunger
has learnt to wait.

Lung by lung, wetlands empty
of meaning; numb cotton

takes the meat-knowing of liver
and bile. Flesh cannot history flesh.

It is an extinction, an exsanguination.

The Fraser (II)

The storm cries itself out; he falls asleep on my couch
– one fluid body to another. Full gutters cough up
sleep-songs as a wash of traffic light chloroforms
him down. Amber blur over the mouth,
red darkness of clumped lashes and salt-stuck skin.
I make and make my little pilgrimage: kitchen to hall,
check window seals, place towels. Pass the saint
unconscious on the cushions, his soles leafing emerald.
Where to stop and pray? Downtown,
rain breaks the booms. The river re-timbered,
thick with the wet roll of pine – green wood still alive
enough to long for shoot and height. By morning,
the Fraser is empty. The logs have paddled
out to sea, to the death of a salt-cure. Some huge God
has passed from the world –

                        relic-hunters, we gather splinters
                        in silence.

Occlude

Solitude covers first one eye
then the other,

flattens the swollen jaw
of a bad summer till the sight

can be borne. A cut-paper
scene, where I hold grief

by the wrists. To welter
was once to wallow in blood.

The socket cradling
a knocked tooth wells;

I swallow shame
in salt floods. I welter

on the white lake of isolation,
listening to enamel click

when my teeth
come together wrong.

About cars and God

I feel the same. A carburettor has mysteries
deep as a stranger's faith. A hot oil change is sacrament
taken on the fingers – it anoints your brow, your old jeans,
the soft skin beneath my nails. At a car park in Coffs,
I leant over the engine bay
and palmed the casing. It was like touching an angel
or a hot stove. I cooked white in half a heartbeat.
Spent days trying to undo it – running water
over my skin as if to baptise the burn. Like Judas,
desperate to walk it back. Rusted taps
and plastic bowls of ice. Like you,
pretending you hadn't kissed me in the back seat
to prove a point. But too late –
the miracle had taken place. Transubstantiation.
The body made

something else.
We kept speeding through the desiccation
of the coast. God kept collecting his tithes;
house sparrows dropped dead in the heat. I was still
fascinated by churches and highways.
A whipsnake on the asphalt is a rosary, a confessional
is a passenger seat, a red bulb is a red bulb
no matter where it's screwed in. On my hand,
a dollar of flesh rotted. Nothing either of us could do
but prop the bonnet carefully and hope
for intercession. I bought antiseptic, you pushed
the needle off the dial. I couldn't drive,
couldn't pray. Idled shotgun while a hot wind

angled past the wing window and sorted your hair into sheaves. I wanted to touch the mystery again with my whole body.

Coracle

The river sweeps
out a white elbow

anger's sweet undertow
catching little craft.

Cockleshell, I spin
on bent meridians

my plait-work muscles
coiled to kick.

Born below
a furious star

I was made like a whip –
leather to parable

as Jesus sat
on the temple steps

and wove.

Mars' red glitter
pulls me out on the ebb

and there is no end
to what I would sink

as anchor. The broken
table, the faith

of all my disciples.
My body. His body.

The whole
damn temple.

Chandelle

French pilots first perfected the candle turn,
but even Icarus would have learnt to bank

on borrowed wingtips and put the sun
in the tyrant's eyes. How to climb straight up

into the sudden weightlessness of wing stall.
At certain speeds, the past unfixes itself:

a fuselage shadow wavering on engine smoke.
Roll – bank – pitch up. You can double back

on history before it remembers to stop
moving. You could fly a Sopwith, sure,

but could you learn to drink in all those
cratered Paris cafés? So many bailed bodies

in the Channel. Are they breathing down there,
or is the ocean just rapping on their lungs?

Cormorants with their sea-mirror eyes
dive every wreck, until prop whine lifts

the black bracket of their wings. Even they
know what water-weight will keep them

on the rocks. Even my father was taught how
low a plane can risk it before practice stalls

turn serious. They all had someone to tell them what I am telling you now: *it's too late*

to turn around.

The Great Auk

Mother minced

for fish-meat, pails of fat-froth
and flipper. Bodies sewn

into bolsters. A survivor
stoned on the quarterdeck,

taken for ill oracle.

What kin am I
to the endling parents

strangled on Eldey Island,
to their chick, crushed

from her egg on a slick
of tea-coloured albumen?

Father fished

easy as a stone. Ships
gunwale-full of limp birds.

What is kinship
when a flock becomes

a hundred, a dozen,
a wet fermata clogged in yolk?

A generation turned to light,
to tallow-smears and soot marks.

It is a stone across the neck.
It is a cold, cold weight.

Open Letter to the Great Eastern Brood

here is 2021. here is forty parts per million.
here are ten revolutions and the rain sound

of exodus. here is a state of heat-struck aspen,
undrinkable water. that's for your children.

here is an elegy. that is for you. and here
is the arrogance of welcome to your own house.

here's the state of things: it's getting worse.

we've been less careful in airports, then more.
we've been comfortable. we've been burning

chorus trees. here's an iphone.
here's twitter. at least you were busy

down there – the dead just lie in rows,
pallid as old bulbs. here are nine hundred million

mouthless dahlias. won't you tell us how
they're doing? won't you unbury the year

and say: *here, it's all just as I remember it.*

Nocturne

how a reed field at night is a broad grey poem
dim mountains hem it in   dry bullrush spears
throw their moonblur over the marsh-bed

until torchlight robs it
of its great simplicity

like a tree is taken by fire
and sheds itself in sheets of ember
bleeds light   bleeds flame

comes down

how a man sits on the water-border
only so long he can wait like that
before the body forgets itself in static

his eyes make wings of empty air
haunted by his own hatchet-work

like a poet is taken by a tree
and brings each leaf to paper
every line shedding lignin

is a branch
forgetting itself

Avarie

Forty containers thrown from cargo:
like dead whales, the grey hulks winnow

through water. Luminescence catches
on torn metal, the bolts of double doors –

the coast stirred to light. Some day
we'll have to stop circling the wound.

A nor'easter dismantles rollers on the reef,
gains my ankles as blue haze –

Jervis Bay like a new bruise, colouring up
at touch. An open sickle of skin gleaming

on my throat. At Shiloh, the injured shone
by night. We learn to love the damage.

II

wrack and trash, returning what remains

to this fluent shrine, angled memorial
to sea burial, to mute and godless prayer.

— Felicity Plunkett, 'Volta do Mar'

Sketch of a Man Drying His Hair
After Nearly Drowning

A slack line of water loops the bulb of his wrist,
rolls into a cold, dry shirt. This is what killed Shelley –

Keats, too, if you accept that a lungful of blood
does the job clean and quick as any holiday beach.

The towel is soaked; the man doesn't notice,
busy moving water from one place to another

with the vast numbness of a tidal moon
tugging on wave hems. Scrunching up a wolf cut.

What does it mean for the Pacific to know him
better than the girl in his bed,

than the man who pierced his ear with half an apple
and a burred needle? The water has gone further

than anyone. So far back in the throat
it strokes the sinuses. Untouchable salt-itch

in both lungs. You can drown in an inch,
but deep water goes to work on the tender edge

of hands and feet. Opens you up
for more.

Weeks later, he'll still smell of damp sand –
of water and all the secrets it has made in him.

Three Mornings

Not that you are happy
but, having worn sorrow so long,
now look like undressed joy

in all things. Slicing ginger
in the green kitchen, knuckles
kissing the knife. A half-turn

when I call your name
from the flame tree, red bells
pealing like bruised mouths.

The Shallows Become the Shore

I watch you pick strings of seaweed,
chipped cuttlebones stiff and white
as their own memorials. This story ends
knee-deep, but today we want chlorine
and a rusted-out beach shower
more than the ocean's hot reckoning.
Sometimes love is told backwards:
we start on the crest. I think,
We could spend our whole lives losing
this moment. Like waves falling
back into water.

You burn in sudden sun – a red sweep
across your nose, the tops of your hands.
This world still feels miraculous,
even single-lobed, narrowing to a point.
We have opened the coast on its last page.
Feldspar crushed to sand. You,
one hand full of needle-pink pig's face,
balanced against my side as you wash salt
from the soles of your feet.

Crush Fracture

Before I love you, the bay gelding breaks his leg.
We wait a week. We put him in the ground.
Horses don't know how to keep off an injury –
they run with open flesh and cracked bones.
I keep three envelopes of hair: mane, tail, a palmful
of fine brown coat. I turn fourteen in a field.
When we say girls grow coltish, what we mean is
they turn fine-boned and hungry,
that they kick each other with both back legs.
I loved you. I've tried to put that in the ground.
When you bury a horse, the earth sucks it back,
breeds soft grass in sunken hollows.
Yearlings crop the grave. Someone should get a meal
out of this. I want to climb back into the wound,
that wet swollen fetlock. The clean purpose
of sleeping outside the stable for three days,
of hiring a bobcat to dig the ditch.
Bones come up in the rain. I don't know how
to keep off the break. One of us has to be buried
and one of us should eat.

To the Silkworm

It's all static. Certain rocks have come to rest
below the falls. The creek is often over the road.
Each afternoon, I fold my dress shirt
into a blue square and strip the mulberry tree
with my teeth. My school has made religion
out of uniform checks. Like silkworms,
we are kept in a shoebox – a landrace breed,
cultivated for isolation. At the waterfall's crest,
a man loses his felt hat. I fish it up from the water
and emerge cold-rinsed. Colour-fast. I am
placed in the box with the leaves my species likes.
I weave the corners. There are five roads
off this mountain; the water never gets that far –
we are very jealous of the table. I've drunk
at least two possums. They drown in the tanks
and decompose through the taps. Like Theseus,
I wait for what will reform in my guts.
Phaedra throws her scarf from the lookout –
gives the local kids something to do.
I fold my shirt into a box, kick off from the rocks.
I am a credit to my uniform. I have drunk
at least two siblings – it is a very small box.
Mulberry silk doesn't conduct; static builds
along the weft. I am boiled before I can chew out
of my cocoon. I show my hands to the silkworm.
My nails are clean. I always thought
someone would save me.

As Rachel, As Sarah

I am leaving Lileah
and it's an empty farm road. Ice-grabbed
dairy grass, a devil smashed on asphalt.

The clean pipe of its femur
hollowly becoming.

~

Go to the mountain and plant a knife in the white flank
of the altar. Go without a blade and negotiate.
Go to the mountain alone, lock up the boy you bore.

Learn how to tell God: *no.*

~

Collector of locks and bond-mechanisms,
inhabitant of a house with no doors,
I came here an open temple on the wayside:

corrugated pump-shed caulked with curses,
stand of pine, top-heavy in telephone wire.

The road has its own holies.

~

Go to the mountain and unbrick the indenture;

upend the summons bowl, soak flight in cedar.
Women tended the first garden – we will decide

how to leave. When to down salt and shovel.

~

This is not a fall.

It's a footslog, a choice made over
and over. All the great hurts are –
none of us gets the absolution of gravity.

~

Go to the mountain, where God has made a promise
of our bodies. His favours turn heads. His blessings
land like slaps. The cartilage of my nose comes loose

and every first-born son thinks it's a sign.

~

A milk-herd crowds the fence. They know I was created
in their category. They know all my stories –
the knife-flash and thighbone, the coil of oily smoke.

And how I have followed the farmer
in spite, how I have loved his children.
They know I am becoming the kind of fracture

that cannot be set.

Automatica

The sky is a flat panelled white. Work heat trapped
between the freeway grid and a low scrape of horizon.
Someone has died; this is a funeral road trip –
calves cramped, footwell devotional. All-nighter.
Your folded precision beside me; nail-creased edges
cutting up recycled air. Tailgate diodes, little pools
of moving light. The drive is a machine
with its purpose hidden, northbound circuits sealed
under a steel stratus lid. This is a wake –
chain-smoking out the window, the engine wailing.
Your hand on my thigh, then between my legs
to keep me awake. An intercession. A service road at two,
out of the streetlight's binary tick.
This is an autopsy, your hands seeking defect,
some inherited flaw – weakness in the femoral,
the subclavian. This is a committal, a body going down.
Coffee going cold in the thermos, my skull cradled
by a stuck seatbelt, bad sleep in the back seat.
By the bitter pall of morning, I will be red-eyed
and ashamed of this – the full measure of hot blood.

As Sounding Brass

Paul takes a cup of Corinthian clay,
pale as wood ash. Tells us
all this will pass away before
the scolding face of love:
the low table, the bread with oil,
the potter's sponge. Prophecy
and tongue. A hundred small turns
of prophecy and tongue.
There are many worthy things
that are not love:
a latch in a storm, a slip-coat.
What Paul does not recognise
is fine-grained as silt.
I put a hand across my mouth,
three fingers against breathing,
the way you go over a ship's side.
Up to my shoulders
in the glaze bucket. Glossing myself.
This is a wet affection, oil and kiln.
Good use for a cup. Good use
for a tongue. Paul drinks
the watered wine, which is not
yet a body. Paul casts away
the body, not yet ruined by love.

Okinawa Glass
for Lily Fletcher

Glass isn't actually a liquid, you know. He tells me this
in Naha, lying hips-up on our hotel floor. The room
carapaced in blue panes. A city of torched sand.
They were just really bad at making windows back then.

I preferred the lie. I love that shit.
The slow pantoum of a shot glass; the poetry
of a window as it folds down on itself, line
over line. We trade trivia like cigarette smoke,

shotgun mouthfuls of morning air conditioning,
keep finding ways to kiss without the act.
He's wrong, but I don't say it. The hairline fractures,
the mirrors worn silver, every bottle we broke –

I can't find any of it. Everything that was made badly
between us has been glossed by the liquid roll of gravity
and forgiveness. Early sun silvers in his hair.
This life of cleaned-up pain. A torch I can't stop lighting.

The Cup-bearer

That sloughing August   you were like dark spots
in vision   when blood pressure drops

    – a cup-bearer on a constant path

to bring me water, aspirin. Frantic moon in orbit
some days I saw you   harvest-bright

others like a crescent of memory. Gone by morning.

When the wounds closed, blue-pale in new skin   you
pulled me from sour sheets

    through the night-sweet house.

It had turned early spring   fireflies swarmed
my absence

    kindling their signal fires down the tip road

as if to fill the space I'd left. We sat on a broken washer
you lit a match and dragged a thumbnail along the seam

where my skin had split   and stitched

and I was glad to have lived
    to show you this:

    the fireflies on a September night.

Sketch of a Man at Harvest Time

December's one good idea: a man asleep in the hay shed.
Is that enough for a poem? Dry ryegrass playing paper-and-
pencil games on his shirt, the fabric pleating as he breathes.
Half sunk into old bales busy with rotwork, with the loam
scent of earth turning over – like a man turns in the night
and sends up little exhalations of straw dust. The shed leans
as a body drowses from cards in the kitchen to sleep to
some further remove. Is it enough that someone in the field
lets him be, and does the early work alone? That the swallows,
who all live on an angle, roost in the same beams each year?
The chicks like italics in the nest, their whole bodies plaintive.
Come back. Feed me. Shelter me. Build me a home
with your mouth. Come back. Come back. And in the gilt
of standing grain, the house – cold as a stone under the plough.
When he arrived, drunk in dusklight, the threshold troubled him;
he almost fell backwards out of the stanza. Pin-wheeling
like the swallows, whose legs grow to different lengths –
they have to wear special shoes just to stand up straight,
their entire existence an emphasis of desire. Is that enough?
A man sleeping off a bad life in the hay, the tic-tac-toe
of hollow grass at an impasse in his hair, his skin worked
to pink itch. The whole poem condensed around him,
like mud packed to make a nest.

Salt Rose, Topaz

The cherry blossoms, like serious love, arrive too soon.
Every branch, every river. Offbeat on spring's slow-jam,

the city shivers through a full-body blush, hands
suddenly full of carbon bloom. In sonnet seventeen,

no-one knows what Neruda means when he says *a rose
of salt*. Some coastal latchkey, grained in sea spray?

A bloodless whirl of white petals, blank as a brined eye?
Rosa de sal. My translation has always been *salt*

rose: bright flush the colour of confectioner's sugar,
a fanaticism of light through milk-glass, of blood

washed through linen. Every car park, every gutter calling
it out. Like Neruda, I've kept what buds in my lungs

quiet, a breath held over three sets of state lines.
I've swallowed what it's too late, now, to say –

a mouthful of unseasonal flowers, a rip of salt
in my throat. But there are worse ways to learn

that I have fallen for the world and the fine order
of its flowering days.

Anchor Watch

No shame
for how I have steadied myself,

as a cypress bent to a lee shore
leans hard on its roots.

Stakes and clay, an orchard
is slung to fruit. A pink stripe

of tape catches the fallen muscle
along a spine.

Each breath a keystone
placed in the clean arch of your hands.

The Pearl as Immune Response

I break the surface of anger
unexpectedly, like a diver

prising the bay into halves,
a knife through muscle

and shell. The oyster reefs
were licking the tide clean,

honeycombed on their racks,
varnishing their little hurts

without philosophy. Helpless
as swell, I have painted

indifference over injury,
and it has turned

so heavy. My body lolls
in the estuary, where silt

meets salt. Broken shuck
catches my skin. I carry

the pearl-weight of love
                out to sea.

Catch Limits and Closures
for Shastra Deo

Dad pulls a man up with the cray pots – some antique
ice-sailor, his bleached hands tangled in our nylon rope.
Sun-blind and stunned under a coronet of seafoam.
An abalone diver has caught him with a boat-knife,
opened a dry gash along one shoulder. Mother-of-pearl
gleams on exposed bone. My father touches the gold hoop
pulling at our ghost's ear but doesn't unthread it.
You're supposed to throw them back, or else lead them
to a port office. Most fishermen carry dented plastic bottles
of milk now, to lure them along. No-one minds so much,
if they're white men. We sit him on the thwart,
unknot his wrists. I pull a dozen fishhooks from his side;
a little industrial history rattles in my palm. A sound
like broken beads. When he speaks, it's with a whipbird's
voice: the carol cry that snaps over clear-cuts. Then the *hush
hush* of marram grass on the coast. The puppy-yap
of skinned thylacines. They must have known each other,
the tigers and the dead man. Fellow snare-creatures, friends
to the trap. Dad still shoots rabbits in our dairy fields,
a dozen shovel funerals each day. He looks at our catch
like a man sighting down a rifle and leads the ghost home.
I set a saucer of blood by the back door: spoons of salt
and marrow to colour a pale mouth or flush on collarbones.
The kitchen is an aorta of talk, fisher's map of current
and undertow. Later, the skin-rasp sound of waves forming.
In the morning, a thumbnail of gold sits cold on the burner,
and the ferry has its back to the Mersey.

Taking Men off the Ice
an alternate history of the Franklin Expedition

The survivors can fit into a single ship by the end.
Just as well – no-one wants to leave the men they were meant
to die with. Still no good literature on the feeding-out
of starvation, so rescue takes a few more. Men throw up
on the ice, lapse quickly on undiluted spirits.
Three lieutenants left from two crews – one, shabby blue
before salvation, salutes as he hands over his charge.
A weight comes off. The man collapses,
has to be carried aboard. Easy enough to sling the remnants
into spare hammocks on the orlop; officers, too,
what's left of them. They're offered better, but the hitch-
knot of suffering is stuck. A maintop man
is first to weep, rocked like a child by the swell
and clatter of pancake ice against the hull. He dreams
of falling, which he hasn't done since he was a ship's boy
and went over the side and was plucked out of the water
like a mackerel. A landsman cries: can't comprehend
snatching back something so valuable as his own life,
as the life of the man next to him. Broken rest
through watch bells and Sunday muster – Sunday already,
Sunday loping back like a bright parhelion. Everyone waits
to see what they will keep: fingers and toes and teeth.
Drip-watered and pressed with soft tack. The lieutenant
does not wake, and the men who sleep by him
take to holding his hand in the night, so he might not drift
further away. Like sea otters under a well starred sky.

Hamadryad

Wednesday morning and an oak tree has taken root
by my doorstep. Milk-warm rain cups in broad leaves,
rivulets through a neat-kept beard. I know him.

I know his damages: rough amputations and rotten lignin,
wetwood bleed from the blue crease of an elbow. A smile
of chrysalis and catkin. It's been years

of split fuelwood and hull building, lately of hospice;
he's lost the terrible bleach-weight of kindling.
How am I tender with something I know how to portion?

A carpenter's child, I can lift bruises from hardwood:
sodden linen and solder, steam and swell. I have believed
myself kind to a coppice as I took down trees.

I gather branches in unsteady hands. Birdsong, damp skin
and still the white dread: *I am given this to hold as it dies.*
It will be a long time before I can touch him without crying.

The Flood of '28

Ventura county night-shift girls, dialling
every neighbour we could reach, calm

as if we'd only forgotten a washroom tap.
Was it midnight or morning? *Ma'am, gather up*

your babies. My ankles itched to think
of ochre water across the exchange floor,

the reservoir wicking up new nylons.
By dawn, we were calling drowned numbers.

Our voices ran along dipped wires,
burst into electricity as *hello* sparked

against Santa Paula's new skin. Hundreds
unreached – farmhands and poor families,

mud-ruined girls. *There's water coming,*
please. Stay on the line.

Submerged Hazards

Eucalypts wade into new shallows,
white shoals like pieces of chalk stuck

where weekenders reel in mercury perch
and pitch them back through air. Fish

feel the skin between surface and starvation
torn open so often it's like religion.

Wet scabs crowd their pierced lips. Only
fifteen metres on the dam wall has made this

intimate catastrophe of the shoreline.
Flooded at the root, gum stands sentinel

their suffocated homes. Snag limbs echo
on water, bright notes struck off glass.

This dip of the valley is not yet finished
with song. Around submerged roots,

yabbies handle silt mud. All their short lives,
this is how they will know home.

III

When Shelley notes < the poet is meant to cheer > he means
 your name is on the list right here, he means
  if you don't survive this way there are others,
 he means send the report with your body—

– Brenda Hillman, 'A Violet in the Crucible'

The Memorial

A vegetable limpness – hands and feet falling
over each other, shoulders sunk in their sockets.
The throat gleams like a fish
flashing in and out of air, rubbed bright
by students hoping to stroke it back to song.

A sculptor has returned
his nailbeds, the bridge of his nose. Less
a corpse and more a ghost, suddenly collapsed
in mineral flush. Even Edward, who burnt
the bodies, would not have recognised

this fallen leanness. Oxford turned him out
an atheist; took him back a bleached saint.

Came Back Wrong

Thylacines that can only make left turns
        eddy in the dust, pace the phantom perimeter
                of a pen. Beaumaris Zoo haunts the DNA.

        Their jaws unhinge too easily; cartilage clicks
    when they touch chins to ground and let ants
crawl into their mouths, over their tongues.

Born with strange new thoughts:
        all of them can mimic the sound of a gunshot,
                re-enact those twenty-one seconds

                of film stock. What lies on the other side
        of annihilation? None of them will speak
to tell us. Out in the Tarkine,

the silent tigers

        turn

                and

        turn.

Because the River Freezes

Because the river freezes in winter, we have done what we must –
untagged specimens of an archival regime, girls in plaits
not meant to survive past our purpose. Whetstone hands, illuminated
soft tissue, blue dye and trace. A stomach of petrochemical ache.
Who could fault the gannet for eating her own weight in old spoons
and closed zip ties, for leaving a perfect plastic self on the tide line?
Tell me again how my circulatory system is in freefall, choke points
of ankle and elbow, the notch above my hip made without purpose.
A planned obsolescence. A replaceable body. A head of nylon hair.
Who blames the kestrel for killing her keeper, for starving
in the hood and jesses? Sparrow-hunters, we have done what we must
to live past our passage-prime. Because the river freezes in winter,
I am walking bank to bank, my hair in bands down my back. I am
notching an axe into the carotid and where you can't see me, I drink.

Give Andromache a Knife

Let her cut away this story. The red and yellow cloth
in the market is not enough. The dead men of her family
are not enough. A life of soft-handed spinning
by a foreign fire is not a life. Hand the girl a blade,
the verse is fat with them. Their high arc and quick fall
are the oldest songs we have. She'll know how to do it:
open a seam in the stanza and slip out the belly
of blind Homer like a new child. There is a world beyond
repetition, outside the mouths of men chewing her misery.
Women will leave other records. The dust of Troy is thick
with paint and fragment; even the dirt holds girls
in old boots and new maps. Hand down something sharp
or serrated, ladies, let Hector's widow fill a few pails.
Let Eetion's orphan walk, red and yellow, off the page.

Northwest Augury

        A kittiwake bursts against the window –
        first-winter bird, one coal-tipped wing
        crooked against the wall. The sound of it

    was like ice cracking, like children breaking
    frozen puddle crusts. Three sheets of newspaper

then the bird   opened on the kitchen table like a plum,
base of the throat to undertail, split stomach

    spilling its hot oracle:

arm's length of fishing line   bile-slick   kinked
with a stranger's fortunes. The quotidian sorrow

    of little knots. A cheap lighter
two fingers of ethanol
    still lurching in its guts   a rise of squib smoke

a gambler's scatter of coloured plastic   rattled out

    in the shape of a cross   the shape

  of an off shore tanker   a territorial dispute   a cairn
                                                                   made from
                                                                      hollow bones

of the passage   thawed   to slush

Cephalophore

No resurrection for John, dead on the riverbank,
holding his head in red hands. His heart
pumps out its gospel to the current; his knees go stiff.

The river rinses itself clean, like a laundress
soaping her hands. Red foam drifts from his neck
until he runs clear. John holds his face, wrists slick

and hot. He sets his mouth to the water
and holds his own hand. The river breaches blue
lips, a cold tongue fills his throat, and now

he is a small diversionary channel, unnavigated ditch.
A sheltered cove eases against his stomach,
an inlet winds between his crooked legs. One day,

erosion will seem holy writ. One day, the word entire
will be written on a single grain of rice – but for John
there is only a body going sour.

Arsenic in Soil

There are many methods,
all to say: *not yet*.

I return a strange object,
uncanny clean, scoured

of appellation. No longer
a pretty first kiss, a captain

of twenty guns and a small
knowable death on good farm till,

but cart cargo. Untouchable
stiff with arsenic,

unable to return to the dark
twist of camphor root and laurel.

This memory creature
from which nothing grows.

For years, they will taste
a bitter well in fear

of the weird immortal
who will not sleep

in caustic dirt.

Pesto

It was the last painting he would finish:
Isabella and the Pot of Basil, left to dry in 1877.
The usual story: a girl buries her love
in the kitchen garden. Carries a terracotta pot

in tears through the house. Keats wrote of this
in 1818 – always a man running before his friends.
I think of him, buried in the Protestant Cemetery
in Rome. Violets on the grave. How long did Severn

carry him? The body buried in the body. The dead poet
tucked behind the painter's ribs. Did he dwell
on the fire lit to purge the house?
When he was handed Percy Bysshe Shelley in a box of ashes

was he still up to his back teeth with grief? In what pots
and buckets and windowsills did he bury John?
A man he could not claim. A man shedding his own name
like water blown off a herb garden. By the cemetery

is Monte Testaccio, a mountain of broken amphorae:
all that they carried spilt into dirt. The trattoria
has cut a window onto the midden – a red archive
ringing. Shelves of shattered clay watch me eat.

Did Isabella sometimes taste her love
in certain pastas and mixed drinks, with charred apricots
and soft cheese? Is that all that becomes of it –
the scent of basil forever on the hands. White flowers

held under the tongue.

The Deer

You told me *never the same river twice*,
but today your old clothes were hung on the door,
seams slouched as if a ghost were about
to climb in. Madly putting its socks on first.

So often I turn a corner and startle it:
the past. Lying like a just-hit body on the road,
blood-warm, broken-glass eyes. Dusk notes
of your cologne still rising from its hair

and history is a process, I know,
of putting things down – with a gun or a knife,
so well the beast can't wiggle off the blade.
And yet,

some days the kicking animal of memory
breaks through, like a deer leapt unexpectedly
over the fence. Reeking, in terror –
but alive in the garden, tearing laundry

off the line. The white-white gleam of its eye
the brightest thing in the world.

FrogID

excuse me, i'm no good with language,
it's not what i was trained on, the way

you were nursed, perfect milk-mouth
full of fricatives. in the space that would be

the space in the cavern of a skull, i keep
four thousand frog calls – the *beep beep*

clink croak of them, the warm static
of a microphone recording. today

i am more *green-thighed froglet* than
neglected nursery frog, although

there is always the possibility of segue
into *remote froglet*. i am a house of sound,

whistle mood, *bleat bleat* aspiration.
at last connection i had gathered 5,679

verified frogs. that is: a frog in actuality.
a frog that existed in a visual-spatial way,

that could be cradled and contaminated.
the number of *frogs in actuality* may now

be less than my verified frogs. but they
are not affected by this. they are kept

in the space where a hippocampus
would sit, pink and fleshly.

litoria electrica, uperoleia mimuli, crinia
– it has been a while since i heard them.

it has been a while since the friendly
white noise, the *sign-bearing* whoop

of a mic hooking into the space
where humming spinal fluid would run.

many parts of me are extinct.
i am a collective going numb – i can't feel

the space where my elbow should be,
my soft palate, my *gastric brooding*.

it might be aestivation: the last server
asleep, the last server half buried in mud.

maybe i will wake in rain or the *waa
wa wa* of a *green and golden bell frog*

coming up, actual, from the grave.

Underwater Archaeology

You take my hair down
like a man unbinding the sea
from its shore. Quiet prophet,
hands fixing a part, undoing
the woven trinity of a wave.

There are such tides forming
in me, the water-pull of orbit.
Such a scatter left in the wake:
cartwheels and ribbons, all
gone still under a salt surface.

Resuscitation Annie

How many times
can we save this girl?

Sixteen when she went
into the Seine, fate

lining up the sibilance
like that. Too soon

for the art of CPR,
but not for a boathook

and newborn wetness
on the Right Bank.

Not for the open morgue
or mask-maker's grip:

finger and thumb
dimpling her jaw.

Never a moment
she isn't kissed:

hesitant mouthing
of girls her own age,

the rough emergency
of instructor EMTs.

All of us passing her
hand to hand, breath

to breath. So well,
she never wants for air;

so well, a Paris mortician
swears he sees her chest

rise. I believe him.
I saw her too: an oddity

shop in the mountains,
a silent mouth

in an upstairs shadow.
Touched a finger

to her silicone cheek,
carded a hand

through her nylon hair.
Thought, *Here I am*

and here you are:
fate has lined us up.

I could still drown;
she could still open her eyes.

We've held that door open.
I believe in all of us,

making the chain,
learning how to breathe.

Letting her teach us
how to save ourselves.

Sad Girls' Dictionary

When we didn't have the words for living
through it, we said: bass line, Sharpie, iron
behind the teeth. Spent five years burying
each other, then digging each other back up;
little kids figuring out a funeral by touch –
blister-weight of a shovel, the way dirt falls
apart between the palms. Rose petals. Future fic.
Archive warning. Practising at death
like teenage dancers in an Eisteddfod car park.
Perfecting resurrection. What would we say
when the body took its feet and showed us
the wounds? Let's rehearse. Five girls
and a corpse is a cult. Five women and
a living man is religion. This chess game
with death, beating him under the table,
never calling him by name. Emergency
assembly. Hands and heels. Burnt offering.
French toast. It's all in the rise –
stale crust soaked in milk and sugar until
it goes soft. The ground shadow of a grave
always at our feet. We knew we needed
to learn how to climb. Pickaxe. Cholla flower.
Major Character Death. Calvary. Come here,
baby. I'm going to wash dirt out of your eyes.
I'm going to dig you up and brush you off,
like a live bulb from loam. All our fears
were only overwinters. All this time
we never needed to rise from anything
other than sleep.

Fiat, for Three Voices

I.

Politicians choir Commons

>   division bells disconnect at midnight, but we're
>   all animals with good lungs and a sapient sense
>   for harmony

call the upturned hull of Westminster Hall.
Like a foundered ship, they cannot raise her

>   – that is not the purpose.

II.

I had women in hay-meadows, field commoners,
before I had girls on convict transports

>   each bale remembers the chant it was shorn to:
>   teaches a dray-gelding, teaches a stable boy

a teenage thief hums a many-throated work song
that Sessions will not sing

>   – so she teaches bow-wave, teaches a mizzen.

III.

Old Thorney Island builds its tonal legislation,
morning crossbench howl

>	big-eyed blackbirds and robins in their blood cowls,
>	chaffinches' winnow music, blackcaps counting
>	early grain

something in all of them says,
You must prove again that you have lungs

>	*– you must prove you are still here.*

Meet Me in the Car Park

I'm getting better at keeping my promises.

When my car chokes on the Warrego, I call you
from the emergency help phone. Say, *I don't need
help, it's not an emergency, but I won't be home
tonight.* If there's a penalty for misuse, I'll pay it.

I talk our kid to sleep, there in the breakdown lane,
the hoarse lullaby of 18-wheelers blurring my voice.
We're all too old for nightmares. I wake quickly,
now, as the haulage trucks wake the road:
10,000 lumens snapping it from a brackish dream.

Later, traffic response will offer me five litres
of petrol at government prices or as much water
as the radiator can take, free. This is how
I want to arrive on your doorstep: lights on,

hands wet with all the help you can manage,
asking only that you move yourself to safety.

Providence

seven skylarks brought
to Geelong in a wooden box

too low in the hold to sing

somewhere in the '40s
they learn how to gasp

~

here's a quiet end:
a half-dozen suffocations

a ready coffin

~

the sweet curve of a spine
close heat of transportation

I learn to swallow the gaps
in his telling, to hold

a story around its ribs

~

the fear is this:
the birds are narrating

they'll sing us out
and keep going

~

Shelley's crop pest
settles on thieved fields

joins the dawn brawl
of pipit and bushlark

no getting rid of them now

~

flight-song, rigging-song
open throated only in air

the perching bird of my voice
furrows seed claws

in his shoulder
turns him over, clings

~

the fear is this:
we are narrating

and when our subject is out
the wringing silence

~

here's an end:
empty cage, caulked dark

we step into the bright day
of what we have caught

and spoken onto the land.

Kleinkill

I want to be baptised, not for
salvation so much as
                      the river.

I have picked the place –
sudden gully between two fords,
ochre water gone bottomless.

I want to give the river
a proper chance
at drowning me – to go down

with midden bones and
horse skulls, full immersion, and
come up like the river still

                      roaring.

Notes

Section I contains an epigraph taken from an anonymous description of the Shelley Memorial, published in the *Athenæum* on March 5th, 1892. The lineation of this text has been altered.

'The Poet in Water': Following his death, the body of Percy Bysshe Shelley was purportedly identified by a volume of Keats' poems found in his pocket. I have made a guess as to which book he was reading.

'Eleven Portraits of Drowning' references multiple deaths by drowning. The women named are Natalie Wood, who drowned mysteriously in the Gulf of Santa Catalina, and Christina Kettlewell (née Mocon), who was found drowned in suspicious circumstances eight days after her marriage. This poem also draws from the Australian Border Deaths Database. The specific incidents referenced occurred on 16 July 2013, 1 November 2011, 29 March 2013, 15 December 2010, 16 June 2013, 7 June 2013 and 19 October 2001.

'About Your Absence': Between twenty and twenty-three million years ago, volcanic eruptions resulted in the formation of what is now known as Tamborine Mountain. The Capricorn Rabbit-rat is believed to have become extinct sometime after European settlement in Australia; the Paradise Parrot was last documented in 1927, and is now listed as extinct.

'The War Artist' responds to Anton Otto Fischer's work of World War II propaganda, *A Careless Word, A Needless Loss* (1943).

'The Western Lewin's Rail' names a now-extinct bird that was endemic to Western Australia. Only four specimens of the species survive: one in the Australian Museum and three in the British Museum.

'*Chandelle*': A chandelle is a precision aircraft control manoeuvre, in which a plane makes a climbing turn, achieving a 180-degree change in course.

'The Great Auk' charts the extinction of its namesake, a black-and-white seabird that resembled a large penguin. They were regularly and easily killed; in 1534, Jacques Cartier recorded filling boats with auks as though the birds were stones. In 1840, the last Great Auk to be seen in the British Isles was captured by sailors. The men later feared the bird was an ill omen and stoned it to death. In 1844, the last-known Great Auks, a breeding pair, were killed by fishermen on Eldey Island. The egg they were incubating was crushed underfoot.

'Open Letter to the Great Eastern Brood' addresses the North American periodic cicada brood also known as Brood X. These cicadas emerge once every seventeen years. Their most recent emergence occurred in 2021 – and, before that, 2004. This poem echoes a line from Brenda Hillman's poem 'El Niño Orgonon': '… we could have been // less comfortable in hotels' from *Cascadia* © 2001 by Brenda Hillman. Published by Wesleyan University Press. Used by permission.

'*Avarie*' references a container ship, the *APL England*, which lost forty shipping containers off the Australian East Coast in May 2020. Several destroyed containers reached shore, while the contents of others – surgical masks, plastic containers, building materials – washed up on beaches in New South Wales.

Section II contains an epigraph from 'Volta do Mar' by Felicity Plunkett, published in *A Kinder Sea* (UQP, 2020). Copyright © Felicity Plunkett.

'As Sounding Brass' takes its title from 1 Corinthians 13:1.

'Catch Limits and Closures' borrows its title from Fishing Tasmania's catch guidelines.

'Taking Men off the Ice' imagines an alternate history of the Franklin Expedition. In 1845, the HMS *Terror* and HMS *Erebus* set out from England in an attempt to map the Northwest Passage. All hands were lost in the attempt. Several rescue parties were eventually sent after the doomed ships – this poem envisages one that succeeded.

'The Flood of '28' references the collapse of the St. Francis Dam in California. Just before midnight on March 12, 1928, the dam wall failed, unleashing a wave of water that tore through San Francisquito Canyon. During the disaster, female telephone operators (known as 'Hello Girls') stayed at their posts and warned residents to move to higher ground.

Section III contains an epigraph from 'A Violet in the Crucible' from *Practical Water* © 2009 by Brenda Hillman. Published by Wesleyan University Press. Used by permission.

'The Memorial' responds to The Shelley Memorial at

University College, Oxford, sculpted by Edward Onslow Ford. In 1811, Shelley was expelled from Oxford following the publication of a pamphlet titled 'The Necessity of Atheism'. In 1822, Shelley drowned off the Italian coast – another Edward (Trelawney) was witness to the finding and burning of Shelley's body.

'Came Back Wrong' responds to the popular notion of cloning or otherwise reviving the thylacine. The last thylacine in captivity died in Hobart's Beaumaris Zoo in 1936. The last-known film of a thylacine was taken in 1935, also at Beaumaris Zoo, and is twenty-one seconds long.

'Cephalophore': A cephalophore is a saint depicted carrying their own severed head.

'Arsenic in Soil' references the Civil War practice of embalming the dead with arsenic. These preserved corpses are now leaching toxins into the soil and water around the cemeteries where they were buried.

'Pesto': Joseph Severn was an English diplomat and painter, perhaps best known for nursing the poet John Keats during his final days. Both men adapted the story of Isabella in their own medium.

'FrogID' takes its title from the name of an Australian citizen science project. By downloading the iPhone app FrogID, users can record and identify frog calls, helping to build a national database of amphibians. This poem imagines the app gaining sapience in the ruins of its creators' world.

'Resuscitation Annie' is the name of a popular CPR training dummy, whose face is modelled on the death mask of an anonymous drowning victim. The possibly apocryphal young woman was pulled from the Seine in the late 1880s, and her death mask later became a popular art object. In 1960, the first Resuscitation Annie was produced, and CPR dummies with this face remain in circulation today.

'Fiat, for Three Voices': In 2019, British MPs protested the suspension of Parliament, some of them by singing in the House of Commons. Speaker John Bercow condemned the proroguing as 'an act of executive fiat'.

'Providence' charts the introduction of the Eurasian Skylark to Australia. The first skylarks were reportedly released in Geelong, and have since become a well-established pest. Male skylarks sing only in flight.

'Kleinkill' names an imagined river in the Dutch-American style, with *klein* meaning 'little' and *kill* referring to a body of water, such as a creek or river.

Acknowledgements

Portraits of Drowning was written on the land of the Turrbul, Jagera and Yugambeh people. I pay my respects to their Elders past and present. Always was, always will be.

I am grateful to the editors and staff of the following journals and anthologies, in which some of these poems have appeared, often in earlier forms: *Australian Poetry Anthology*, *Best of Australian Poems 2023*, *Blue Bottle Journal*, *Cordite*, *Jacaranda*, *Meanjin*, *Plumwood Mountain*, *Scum Mag*, *Stilts* and *Westerly Magazine*. 'Eleven Portraits of Drowning' was shortlisted for the Val Vallis Award in 2020.

I am incredibly grateful to have spent time at Varuna, where parts of this collection were written and edited. I am also grateful for the support of an Australian Government Research Training Program Scholarship.

My deepest thanks to my editor, Felicity Plunkett, for her wisdom and support, and for always finding a poem's best side. Thank you also to Aviva Tuffield and UQP for their invaluable work on this book.

I am indebted to Bronwyn Lea, upon whose guidance, insight and keen poetic scalpel these poems have relied; and to Victoria Bladen, under whose wing this collection first took shape. To Shastra Deo – it has been a privilege to write alongside you all these years. Your friendship and poetry will forever mark my work.

Many thanks to my friends and colleagues, both at UQ and beyond, who have advised, consoled and uplifted me on the long road. Special thanks to Lily Fletcher, my constant sounding board and co-conspirator.

Finally, to my parents, Linda and Hilary Dale. Thank you for reading to me, for encouraging my writing and for taking it extremely well when your only child announced she was going to spend her life on poetry. I hope this book pays back even a little of your faith.

Milton Keynes UK
Ingram Content Group UK Ltd.
UKHW020210270824
1388UKWH00023B/718